Additional Praise for *cue*

"The poems in Siwar Masannat's *cue* constantly find a place of necessary
disquiet in the interaction of the personal and intimate, and the broader
political realities of danger and concern. There is a sensuality in the manner
in which they offer lyrical expressions of desire and possibility. Yet, always
lurking in the shadows are the threats to desire, communication, and affection.
These are the things that demand the language of "codes," the secret idioms
of connection necessary in "hostile light." As a result, Masannat's poetry
keeps pushing its way towards forms necessary to articulate increasingly
challenging realities in the world. Terms like "hybridity," "experimentalism,"
and all the derivations of the prefix "trans"—transcultural, transnational,
translation—richly and beautifully preoccupy Masannat. Even as these poems
are equally compelled by a desire to communicate—sometimes in blunt
witticisms, sometimes in song, and sometimes in lyric vulnerability.
cue is a stunning second collection by this exciting poet."
    —Kwame Dawes, author of *Sturge Town*, Norton 2024

Previous Praise, for *50 Water Dreams*

"How rare and exhilarating it is, in our time, to find a book that is both wildly
inventive and daring in its style and incredibly compelling in its content!"
    —Ilya Kaminsky, author of *Deaf Republic*

"These clips of language beg for recovery, for coherence in a world unlikely
to cohere. 'What is causality, / for x to lead to y? What / is loss of land?'
asks Masannat in *50 Water Dreams*, her essential debut."
    —Sally Keith

"*50 Water Dreams* beckons us into a mysterious world of broken tesserae,
a dispersed mosaic the reader must puzzle over to reconstruct. What we
discover, as the pieces begin to fit, is that Siwar Masannat subversively flips
the script of scripture, and invites us to re-read what we thought we knew
as the story of a land called 'holy.'"
    —Philip Metres

Also by Siwar Masannat:

50 Water Dreams

CUE

GEORGIA REVIEW BOOKS

edited by Gerald Maa

CUE

POEMS

SIWAR MASANNAT

The University of Georgia Press   *Athens*

Published by the University of Georgia Press
Athens, Georgia 30602
www.ugapress.org
© 2024 by Siwar Masannat
All rights reserved
Designed by Erin Kirk
Set in Baskerville
Printed and bound by Sheridan Books
The paper in this book meets the guidelines for
permanence and durability of the Committee on
Production Guidelines for Book Longevity of the
Council on Library Resources.

Most University of Georgia Press titles are
available from popular e-book vendors.

Printed in the United States of America
27   26   25   24   23   C   5   4   3   2   1

Library of Congress Cataloging-in-Publication Data

Names: Masannat, Siwar, author.
Title: Cue : poems / Siwar Masannat.
Description: Athens : University of Georgia Press, 2024. |
    Series: Georgia
review books | Includes bibliographical references.
Identifiers: LCCN 2023047510 (print) | LCCN 2023047511
(ebook) | ISBN 9780820365978 (paperback) | ISBN
    9780820365985 (epub) | ISBN 9780820365992 (pdf)
Subjects: LCGFT: Poetry.
Classification: LCC PS3613.A7927 C84 2024 (PRINT) |
    LCC PS3613.A7927
(EBOOK) | DDC 811/.6—dc23/eng/20231012
LC record available at https://lccn.loc.gov/2023047510
LC ebook record available at https://lccn.loc.gov/2023047511

CONTENTS

cue includes photographs from Akram Zaatari's art project *Hashem El Madani: Studio Practices*. Zaatari's work came to my attention in 2017 in Amman and, fortuitously, I heard him speak in 2018 at Darat al Funun. In his lecture, Zaatari defined an art object 'conscious of its history,' emphasizing how the transactional nature of studio photography enables a photograph's historicization too. *Studio Practices* as an art project excavates photographs from Hashem El Madani's studio from the period between the 1940s and 1970s in Saida, Lebanon. Excavation as an artistic technique appears especially significant in Zaatari's oeuvre, including his films.

In *Studio Practices*, we witness a visual local and transnational modernity, from portraits of Palestinian resistance fighters, to people posing next to radios, to photographs of naked newborn babies. Photographs of 'same-sex' weddings appear alongside the legible queerness of a tailor called Ahmad El-Abed. These performances, mimicking heterosexual cinematic love scenes, emerge in relation to the respectability politics of the moment—heterosexual couples and unrelated men and women are not supposed to display public intimacy. The homosocial and queer, then, intermingle in a visual fabric that is playful and ambiguous, engaging disguises and displacements. The word queer is here a translation too. Like all translations, it invites questions of transmission as a nonlinear, self-reflexive process.

Responses to Zaatari's project have mirrored his approach of excavation and layering. Gayatri Gopinath emphasizes that the queerness of Zaatari's project is multiple: it emerges in the subjects' performativity, staged and/or organic; in the positioning of Saida as a city in an "outsider" region to Lebanon's national discourse by virtue of Saida's historical relation to Palestine, interrupted by Zionist settler colonization, invasions, and occupation; and in the desire that drove Zaatari to choose particular photographs over others. In an interview with Zaatari, Chad Elias emphasizes Zaatari's own desire for the male body and for subjects' performances of hypermasculinity, calling his process a "deployment of the archive as a site of libidinal investment." And Tarek El-Ariss, in an essay about the project, offers close readings of a number of photographs to reveal their staging. Their voices all inform or appear quoted in *cue*'s arrangements.

Free Palestine.

CUE

for a moment

the world in her deep
burdensome sleep
loved us almost
as wide as our creator did

the opaque weight

of birth

whole

long   heart

a theology

of nature.

3

my father is sheikh mohammad el madani, a religious authority.

he was asked once: your son is practicing photography. isn't it a sin?

he said: when one stands near a pool of water and sees one's reflection in it, this is photography. there is no harm in it.

this is not a sin. this is a transfer of an image.

the sun is a camera which operates only in black and white. no vase nor vessel fit to an entire flower's spirit. still in a world kin to *the flower world* we could share a planet or a lilith or their acquaintance and we as necessary *refuse to translate.*

tarek el-ariss writes *that it is difficult not to consider death as a possible culprit in the abandonment of these pictures.*

in *tales of the waria,* mami ria says there is *no pain worse than losing your husband* (of a dozen years or so) and she is ever dignified, mami ria, grieving in grace in the cool of his sudden absence.

whereas asmar here is the true melancholy center of the photograph—*star* of a delicate, plastic flowering—najm's soft lean into him is as tender as i recollect your hands: gentle, warm—generous on my knee.

we

imagine you're a male garter snake just waking up in the spring. you're chilly and covered with cold dirt and mud. you see a spot of blue sky through the ceiling. you crawl out and are greeted by the smiling faces of ten horny males hoping you're a female. you're not. but they're hot and fast, and you're cold and slow. wouldn't it be nice to roll around in the sun—why not use some perfume to signal your intentions? and if you're one of the ten males watching this face poke up through the ground, and you see he's not the female you were waiting for, why not welcome him into the sunlight and get acquainted?

thamnophis sirtalis parietalis:

تُزهر ياسمينة زرقاء
فجأة أصبح أنا الأفعى وأنت ثعبانًا
رباطنا على خواصرنا

وأنت مرحُ حفلتنا الراقصة
في حبكة كرتنا تأتيني
ثعبانًا وتتركني ثعبانًا

نلعب على طول جسدينا
متطابقان، أهمس لك من جلدي
عن بصيرة ذاكرتها

مربّعة
تلبسنا ولم نلبسها
أبدًا لنخلعها

a bird hits my window, i turn
and my heart for a second stops,

breath delayed at nostril.
muscle and valve will yield

to a common beat once
i hear flapping, glimpse flight

again as glass settles to still.
to love is an entire age of such

rhythm. inventory of vulnerability,
relentless. i laugh at the size

of my worrylove, push it
down to nest in a ligament

at the sole of my foot,
watch it.

the word *disguise* in arabic is *tanakkur,* which
literally means a disowning or a disavowal of
one's representation for the sake of another.
it is sufficient to say *atanakkar,* "i disown," to
mean that one is *in disguise* (el-ariss)

لقد صار قلبي قابلًا كل صورة

we are moving in our experiments toward the new sacredness of
images, we are understanding images to be our equals, having a
life and a power of their own. we make them but they are not
ours. and they are not from us (etel adnan)

وما هي الشمس إلا شمسنا :

sun as androgynous as yellow mixed to blue

tarek el-ariss traces the gazes of those photographed to reveal the hidden hand of el madani in arranging the scene. he points to the desire of the choreographer to see another in a pose—to taste pleasure in the approach, a sincere incline here and another's pursed lips. could the choreographer be an excavator too of the subject's playful desires?

fog-thick morning—

at the party she keeps you company. i love her for a decade running into (an)
other. i forgetful tend to arrive, arrive, arrive without coat—no umbrella or hat
or fish jumping from between my palms. no offering the sea at the edge of your
house a new inhabitant. salt plummets particle by particle from our nostrils. fish
fins plumped by garlic, parsley. between clavicles an owl resides, bartering flight:
for centuries paying its way in weaker prophesies.

i see only
where i now walk. i carry

the tea muddy green. my eggs on me. the owl for weeks hunts down the fish, the coat, the umbrella's wire network. brings dripping polarized salt. these electrons smell, *shifty*, you say. sometimes our body forcefully laid. soon, alone, desire hangs, runs to find night through prayer calls to the nth sun's green light—

>   *my clarity*
with me.

the kitchen here is clean, surface smooth to a squeak. she does not like to
wake up to dirty dishes, glasses, cutlery in sink. if i could, i would screampray
lightning—i owl, i fish, i sheep. i barter beats in the gullet of our sparrow—
asleep across walls, resting till a day new emerges blue—

You
          ah you.

you are the 'effeminate tailor' / i fell for that hairdo your checkered shirts / is that your lover / was he *as honey* did he / steal a kiss on your cheek as you sewed flowers / on his lapel, that lace trim kerchief spilling from his chest / pocket i must confess i am searching for that sugary playfulness / sits like fog over the roof / of my throat / a play by my heart / then my great grandmother / crocheted, sewed, and embroidered intricate / lace only one piece of many pink silk / asymmetrically diamond shaped and round edged / her perfected skill / traveled time from safita to madaba to amman / sits on a small wood and mother of pearl inlay table against the wall in this apartment / imagine her tenderly fierce like the women / i come from / i imagine you might have been fiercely quiet / do you have the darkest eyes of your siblings / some planets we might have at our first breaths align how the universe (re)arranges itself / in the *beekeeper* i read dunya mikhail's telling of how reem the seamstress saved zuhour and her three children / hid them from her father in a room / in a house /

helped smuggle them to safety to zuhour's uncle / years ago i lost any skill of knitting / my (im)patient hands yet / teta and i once made a stuffed doll white cloth green mistletoe / small button face pattern eyes no nose one mouth no gender / teta's singer

machine is no longer sitting on a small table in the second bedroom / were we always coincidental / to each other / i too have the darkest eyes in my family / your sister like you does not smile unlike / you seems uncomfortable in that posture / bending ninety degrees you or el madani chose / for its femininity as zaatari mentions what he mentions (with no judgement) ahmad—i have been heartstretched in place.

my gallantry is such that i wanted to be water.

i encountered one book. i avoided another. i plucked and found myself being plucked.

my left palm only halfway open.

if my seat or leg appear to falter, correct the glasses. ears get tired of extending the eyes' path.

in truth i have never abandoned my foolish, chivalrous heart. for what is gender (v.) in love?

my letter to you is no frame—we exceed it already—as you would have known before i mention what i mention.

when we eat, coquettish around your family. below table finger-
tangle in chicken grease. word impossible in english yet gesture:
you heap my plate full of food.

we aren't looking—teta sneakdrops food onto plates. we
annoyed our no, for seconds or thirds, (un)heard. then she often
says i am unable (to eat or drink), waving crooked hand for no.

jido stops eating in his last week. her appetite grows in her last
years. we stay, attend, wait by bedside or in a room close by as
(s)he is (t)here.

from sydney, she complains: *my husband plans to rear chickens
for eggs.* we divide coop cost over salary. *these chickens strange
or pretty*, fluff feathered, *look nothing like our common
chickens!* she laughs.

rooster by teta and jido's home wakes me at dawn each
childhood weekend— i reluctant cockerel crow call from ear
to windpipe, hoping it reaches you (t)here.

my crone
at dawn like me rises

and me softly knocking for my child
visit, we are all here sitting calm

newspapers with the dead's
names in our hands, radioed

account of those to be buried
lilting and she sips her coffee

and me, my child tea, my uncle
his coffee

and we greet every
day so before most others

حارة

ḥarah

a narrow entrance to a group of houses: family building or two
houses in one stretch of garden: lemon, olive, palms: orchard,
field—children's play territory: ancestor horseman: خيّال (ّ)
apparition: *rode to recover stolen something rode back home*
a beautiful man he was made to marry an ugly sheikh's daughter
so virile he slept with the whole neighborhood: a narrow
entrance to a group of houses: town: city: governorate—he loved
her till the moment he died though she forgot who he was, he
called out for her, cursed a decade of illness, this end: suddenly
sneezed then was gone—he sleepwalked half out of the window:
sleepthought he was protesting—up in (y)our city, no narrow
entrance to a group of houses: stairs: a family building: close to school: a
jasmine tree: بستان: lush garden she later grew inside
the small, enclosed apartment balcony: capital city: central: up
(t)here and (t)here and there—in her town south, a house is
a group of households she the manager of: *the mischievous child*
lurked by the window to the bedroom knowing how it would
drive the man crazy to think one was stealing looks at his
wife: بص: the earth sprouts its first plants: a woman lifts her
forefingers to the sky moving them in prayer: i plant for you,
they plant for you somewhere: حور

eyes of whites so white of black so black of ball so round of lids
so soft so very thin: a neighborhood

chickens were first invented as farmable and companionable x years ago whereas chicken was first itself and then chicken and then hen and cock it has learning abilities that exceed expectations assumed and then discovered to be incorrect by human presiding over the learning of chickens chicken pecking order executed by peck and stare (eye function independent in sides: left = predatorprey and right = pecking perhaps converging for purposes human can identify with) because itself was a fighter low-maintenance bird that cannot fly and some that birth every day human established myriad of relations (and emotions) to chickens at the moment human scientists are working hard to explain the spontaneous biological capacity of some chickens to alter sex

حَبْكة

ḥabka

between story and weave we slight our way in between

gossip and memory, rearrange sound, all (open) secrets of this

and that house. as a house is a circle, motion of rotation—a circle

is all secrets and these dispatch, disattach: same story she told

before she lost grasp of one time and entered another. she said:
jozha majnoun, he beat her out of jealousy.

they all lived in one house that was a group of households she
managed, this one building of overlapping circles.

in *tales of the waria,* suharni's love story fills a chest wide with breath.
to her beloved she says: *your sweet words pierced my bones.*

ahmad, you are living beyond a hundred. we never met no
gestures of yours for me to piece in memory. you only barely
arrange your mouth a smirk is not there but it is possible to see a
shadow mouth i imagine your face's possibilities. perhaps it is
that your eyes betray tenderness only when you are with your
brother perhaps i only imagine that i cannot see that fond flash today.

in our language

فلك

astrology   folklore   astronomy
               girl whose breasts round & balloon

pipe my heart   by your heart   seed
               imperfect(ion)

(t)his body won't do   eddy to (t)his
current   to house to waters
       a (sub)atomic love   beauty
       clove   mole
       right cheek shine in mirror

       tiara: *i was just a place to stop before he found*

                                         a woman

               here is my heart for you
               a ventricle necklace
                  blood center
               an aortic bracelet
                        wear it on your wrist

a sun full of gas and petrol / of fuel oil alcohol and tears

i once fell in love with a woman's eyes for an entire week—i
was delirious with it.

she laughed in chuckles and her chuckles were like fast, soft
hiccups and if sound were *visible,* it would have been, her laugh,
like marbles each one nesting a pastel spiral. the marbles spilling
out from a round center into rows like rays, each bump against
another opening my heart wider and wider though i never did ask
to gather her nor her laughs in my arms.

there is another photographer zaatari mentions who refuses to
hand his negatives to the archives for *he thought that he didn't*
have the right to give pictures of people that had trusted him
with their image to a stranger. he felt that people come to a photographer
because they trust them, so he could not betray his clients.

it has been said in the thieving
language that chickens are cowardly.

this is only true of some.

like people chickens climb and descend
ranks, consort, switch,
and flip and flap and extend

flightless wings. like
people, they get

occasionally peckish.

mama says *the plants they love*
to be near each other, so i let the peace

lily's dramatic leaves caress
the braided slim trunk

of the money tree—its
rust ridden leave tips

i cannot manage to ring back
to health. our home's

balcony through the phone's
screen is more plant-packed

each time we speak—only a single
coffee cup full of vacant space

at the edges of the round
table where orchids sit tall.

then, when baba takes me to visit
the jasmine down by the building's

open gate, my eye grabs that
smallest petal, its absent smell.

kulthoum, what will you visit ahmad el-abed to make? will he
sew for you a pretty, sensible piece—a sheath after the common
cut of today?

as you season the sayyadiyeh do you toss in two lumis? or do
you make do with the tartness of sliced tomatoes?

and have you daydreamed of painting cheeky girls who climb
trees and surveil the most distant edge of the sea?

harjo writes that *the ocean and sky meet out on the horizon for the love*
of touch. to speak like this isn't simplification, or personification for
the sake of making intimacy where there isn't—this is the truth of the matter.

a way that they

pose

the honeysuckle family

my hen mother did not

know I was a two-yolk egg,

did not foresee my shell

ripping her open.

aziz, a farmer in omar amiralay's film *al-dajaj*, says first came
years of drought, weavers-turned-chicken farmers in the village
were all struggling, he adds: *wealth is in the land while chickens fly.*

in bojack horseman's world friend chickens farm food chickens
in *gentle chicken farms* and their slogan is *no one knows chicken like chickens*.

moreno monti and matteo tranchellini photograph the *beautiful*
and they know it chickens and one model is flamboyantly feathered
like a peacock.

according to al-nuwayri, who variably devoured and cited al-watwat,
peahens might leave their eggs for chicken hens to incubate, as peacocks
tend to break peafowl eggs.

amiralay: *were it not for cinema . . . i would not have learned the simple truth that i*
am a part of life, and not the reverse.

gentle chicken farms' advertisement explains the difference
between friend chickens and food chicken just as a disheveled
chicken escapes from *chicken 4 dayz*, a fried chicken restaurant.

when i was a child we would visit the peacocks and ostriches at the
neighborhood aviary. the aviary was home to many monkeys too.

according to monti and tranchellini chickens *were photographed from the side,*
from behind or with only a glance over the shoulder.

the escaped *gentle chicken farms* chicken meets todd and they
love each other. when police come to arrest her he says she's his
wife, she squawks her name: becca, her favorite composer: bach.

chicken farmers in sadad had chicks and chickens listen to the
radio for a duration of 7 days so they would get used to loud
sounds, not get startled if a car passed by.

crow & cockerel got wine drunk one night, cockerel's feathers ruffled & his throat hiccupping, he got foolish: lent his wings to our shrewd crow to fly out & bring more wine. wings exchanged, crow stretched & spread strong cockerel wings, took off, never came back as he had promised. our cockerel waited & waited, comb glistening with wine sweat till he sobered up the following day, his comb dried stiff & red, wings flightless, permanently so.

so they say it may be or may be not each dawn cockerel crows calling for his wings back.

afterwhen she tells me of yasmina and lucy i forget who is the
alpha egg-laying hen

from amman i see them happily pecking in a green blue coop in
sydney

a few months and years in lucy and yasmina switch roles, she
informs me over the telephone

vampire bats big as a plum may feed their whole weight in blood
regurgitate into another's mouth share food groom lick their kin
and friends

leave to fly—

due to a two-yolk egg as it first exits from the chicken it is large
the chicken cloaca narrow an explosion happens bleeding chicken chased by
rest of chickens pecking her eating from her flesh until she dies

the mongoose makes itself very thin, so
that it resembles nothing so much as a piece of rope

some birds defend their entire home range others defend only their food
supply some defend a place to mate the site of their nest

then the snake coils itself around the mongoose

geese mate for life male with male female with male female with male
and male—a male goose deeply grieves after his love dies becomes
despondent, defenseless

the latter breathes in very deeply so that its stomach expands,

sparrows host cowbird eggs in their nests sometimes kill them
sometimes raise them as their own

and the snake is ripped to pieces

we are
(t)here from birth
to self as outside

pulled into what opposite
the ring and roll of

we tongue skin lick
chicken true

to the bone and perverse
our fingers of dead meat

– a chance happening –

'By dint of

knit,

glimmer, sink

a history

by memory,

37

to be the necessary

water,

153

38

winter boot

caked in snow, sweats

salt-dry, straited white

aerial wire to radio

or television, pulled

to roof's pole

irruptive

field

as little as

touch

132

41

the human heart,

without law

bornly slow   stub-

42

you may not know that we're there but we are you
say *i have never seen anything in man and
woman i haven't seen in the male and female
pigeons as though a lion were no more than a house
mouse that roars* rose she says *as i see the shaking of the ben-oil
tree branch by the rain* and the lover he says *i am
better than you because i am above thus i am closer
to the sky* and the lover he replies *i am more humble
than you for i am closer to earth*

how often did you slip into love
as a pigeon in flight enticed
by another pigeon cradled
in a human's hand on the ground?

we

multiplies
skins gods

coined limbs
the art of it

appendages
cut lateral

rogue rouge
bodies we do

peaches pens
appled cheeks

mouths in

I want to be genderless.

now i don't know about you but perhaps say i suffer a lack of
wrist flapping though i might have only ~~imagined~~ felt this wrist

often i = muscular dude i am not
bodied like reesh but you could have
imagined too how i imagine (t)his =
my body

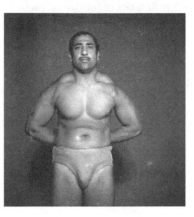

&   huang says about the making
of the film how the warias corrected
her assumptions

   "what for?" one waria asked. for
them, religion was not a source of conflict in
a way that an outsider might imagine.

they suggested a film on a more immediate concern: how to find
lasting love—

         as i sit with my friends last night

love—honest, kind, generous, sexy—is also an immediate
concern

the desire for the photograph, expressed by going to the studio or by inviting the photographer to one's house, is a narcissistic desire coupled with a desire for disavowal in the context of disguise. this is clear from the pictures discussed above. however, what if the desire for the photograph itself becomes compromised? something that could elucidate this reading even further is the fact that none of these commissioned photographs was picked up by the clients (el-ariss).

a deciduous tree
rouged this room

beak against bark
helps her shake
the dead off

for the imaginal to arise

a smokeless cloud emerges in water

& then a bat found

swinging legs

sitting in the corner of a huge owl's eyes—

its origin: the women could not capture the owl
  long enough to mark her eyes in kohl to its very inner edge—

i long to scratch an itch on my old love's right cheek—

the owl only partially caught in flight:

the women then etched a talisman on the left valve of its heart
a muscular room, a beloved's little chamber

i invited the bat to witness me trace circular nodes of my heart,
life, head, fate

lines on my own left hand—

*why not read the many lines and crosses of my indelible heart's
hand?*

spellbound, when we spoke at
all we spoke in code, mouthed

out pomegranates—broken
seeds snapping out of the gates

of our yellowing teeth.
our shadows each

grew plump in longing. we
befriended them and ourselves.

if we simmered
in hostile light we no longer

flinched, nor threw suspicion
back against walls to see

what sticks or grips. we
spilled our fates into

round-mouthed soil beds.
a moment dragging

out of its belly an age before us:
a history waiting to be plucked

clean, like tender lamb's meat
falling off a broken bone.

& bats creased into women—*you cannot fold a flood*—then
women and i in room towards end of wake at night each sat and
a confessional and *why is it that they say (y)our women are
strong?* invisible too

inflected after are—bats in the valley spat out and flew and almost
quickhovered over heads in the pool, and my friend asked
birds, at this time of night? no, bats, no bats, bats. see continuity
of wing to body? asymmetrical hinge to flight's arms.

strange, memory slips out—soundless or pats its opposite—*puts
it in a drawer.* many of them, alternate, not in tandem, each and
together, say this for out of line : in comparison : to whom :
prospective marriages : who perceived :   *listen here*

                         *isn't it known, isn't it, do not rip off my head, i did not first say
                                                      this,* she laughed—

ball in pool thrown and tossed and ridden and i hovered outside
by water edge, sat, stared—she laughed, covered her mouth, they
each at a time spoke or overlapped: *character : sex : beaten :
firsts : education : bikinis : work : control : men*

the women and i some we yawned and some did not speak, some
traded looks, we did not all barter memory, explain, defend, prove
wrong, or break. except my just-dead teta once said *do not
take a man who says no.*

bats dropped from thousands to hundreds—shutter shatter; wave
off, do not swat, flies. i knew she meant *in regards to a notion of
marital permission*—development, a paper explained. bats
vulnerable, bats migratory, bats native, bats most northernly here—

all the dying
petals gather
your names.
i wilt at your
mention, conjure

desire escaping
belly to sound.
i ask those damn
sepals to do
their work:

hold up the dead.
love
by the skin of teeth.
let mine be as sharp
as a cutter bee's

tryst with a leaf,
turning from one solitary
home to another.
let me fill this place
with honey, be

wind to your
kindling, in a moment here
tell me, if i grow you
a fire what care
will i be?

i rise post chivalry
a bare, traveling leg and arm.

i bump against all adjacent
selves i've shed and reworn,

picked up and apart.   where
are you beloved goats and petals?

how do i go with or despite
a paper born of a false boundary's
shameless penury?

as we lean in for a kiss i stab the air with my long tongue

الشغف

how i have always
loved fingers and
looking at them long or
short or pudgy or wild
or neatly hairy or
square—how they
pierce down with knife
a tomato's skin, start
to tighten a bolt before reaching for a wrench, flip pages—even mine

when we make love in the flower world

my heart is close enough to sing

to yours in a language that has no use

for clumsy human words (harjo)

in our language

eyes multiply

a door

هوى

falling   particle
        passion   tumble
           mole
    obsession   mad
       descent :   cavernous
    clavicle   merger
    eyes

clavicleclavicleclavicle

adore

حب

badiou says that to reinvent love is to reinvent life seen through
four eyes (or more)

عشق

we listen: cats, birds to land

ends—you extend your wrist

upright—my heart hops past

        its limit.

my birdheart

      hopper in a hurry

                tends to break

      into a run.

no layoff from this

> desire for the orchid's
>
> purple spots, feel
>
> for thick
>
>
> cream petals.
>
> incline like
>
> an orchid's spike:
>
>
> it roots aerial,
>
> grabs at nothing
>
> but air.

we are all here in this place because we desired it. desired each other.

zaatari: *i would not now take all of those images from someone if i felt they were hesitant to give them. sixteen years ago i would insist, because i was totally convinced that saving pictures is more important than saving emotions and connections with the past. today, i think that saving emotions is more important—especially now we have the technology to digitally scan.*

there is here always a question of consent: means a mystical
belief that you and i consented to being created that you and i as
recipients of the act of creation participated each in a verb of our
own coming to be(ing)

there are days when i (or he) echolocates towards *you* and you
and spirits of beloveds, family

emergence cannot be ruled by the world as we see it
            that what fails

i'm not even telling you what sex i was born as

.

el madani *used a pin to scratch the negatives*

but no love is benign. it can and does engage one's whole being
adnan says

migrating in my heart and despite how saying might make of i
and *you* and you and the women objects in love

men think they own masculinity

adnan says *when in love, one becomes a bird: one stretches one's neck and hears a song not meant to be pronounced. one is speechless*

"her jealous husband,"—

"after she burnt herself to death to escape her misery, he came back to me asking for enlargements of those photographs, or other photographs she might have taken without his permission."

apparition

a stuck truck black
snaps back: red truck

                  in memory

i playful wore

                      a color its like

        i sent a sparrow to you   across mounts

then over these phones   a break of maths our mouths
                              snore and bite

A PLAN(E)T—

that is to say, cells. the small of light bouncing off one lone long hair
from your cheek—that is to say our membranes, the very
operational closure of

the system. here is a bat's long ear and animal
        skin—know that when spallanzani leaned in
        to study flight, he scorched the bat's ear.

am i your wolf, an evolution in which we taste
the tart of sumac to feel its crystal edge?

                      that is to say, the plan(e)t
is at once thirsty and wet—that *operational*
closure of the system, the small of light dying slow on one lone
arm sprouting hair—that is to say, membrane, long fracture.

as i say wolf you must
know that means kin, i will carry you.

                                        so would you
                                   kiss those very

lonely wolves against a crucial step in early
evolution where *genetic progress* long shuns
normative progress?

a system that is to say such *a boundary*

always has a double

function—that lone hair on your cheek in long seducing
wolf loneliness out of me against *a crucial step in the internal
compartment* of grief.

that is to say, we are specialized in plan(e)t
deaths, repeat in the small light oozing from our lone long hands.

beloved, know i will carry your trouble as if it is mine.

a *simultaneous separation from and exchange*

with the environment could be as death-ridden as a cut flower
        drooping slow onto the cool windowsill.

that is to say *progress*, whereas the orchid refuses to
sprout showy in fear of a loneliness, in fear of a cruel singularity
in this house:

long plant *boundary must have been a crucial step in the*
openness of my tongue against your nose hair, that is to say a wolf,
a bat's ear, that is

to hear that a bat's fear is real,
that dog's hiss
at spallanzani's hand—slick—reaching to show once again
how tadpoles grow a new tail.

that is to say, as easy as a mild chicken stew.

the establishment of a lone, long boundary:

      the US military (that contagion) once sought
to weaponize bats'

        echolocation, their smooth flight.
        to 'minimize collateral', they had said.

who is to say the orchid snubs the gardenia's eager flowers?

there, a plan(e)t romance—as if to say *nervous system as criterion* for whose love.

for a pale lone pack hacks away at
something *cellular*

to establish long boundary, membrane.

this wrist of yours is caught in my eye
in a swift, soft flick (you are readjusting
your little watch, instrument of time)

and so i reach for the orchid's root, its
gesture to spiral out.

did spallanzani's hand tremble as he caught
a hint to *progress* in a small bat's ear?

I borrow poetic lines from Etel Adnan's *The Arab Apocalypse*, Emily Dickinson's "You cannot put a Fire out—," Joy Harjo's "This is My Heart" and "earthly desire" from *A Map to the Next World*, and Lorine Niedecker's "Poet's Work" and "Linnaeus in Lapland."

I borrow lines from *Bareed Mista3jil: True Stories*, a cherished collection of life stories and testimonies collaboratively written, edited, and translated by Meem, a queer community organization in Lebanon.

I borrow lines of prose from Etel Adnan's "The Cost for Love We Are Not Willing to Pay," Alain Badiou's *In Praise of Love*, and Dunya Mikhail's *The Beekeeper: Rescuing the Stolen Women of Iraq*.

I borrow conversations from two films and their directors' commentaries: *Tales of the Warias*, a film directed by Kathy Huang, and Huang's article "*Tales of the Waria*: Inside Indonesia's Third-Gender Community" on *Huffpost*; and Omar Amiralay's *Al-Dajaj* and his article "Were it Not for Cinema" published in *Insights into Syrian Cinema: Essays and Conversations with Contemporary Filmmakers*, edited by Rasha Salti.

cue's animals are influenced by the episode "Chickens" (S2E5) in *Bojack Horseman*, by Greg Lanning's BBC film *Chicken Basics: Barnyard Behavioral Science*; and by Mark Lewis' PBS documentary *The Natural History of The Chicken*, and David Korn-Brzoza's *Super Bat*.

The bat appears in al-Nuwayri's *Nihayat al-Arab Fi Funun al-Adab* as having been created by Jesus rather than God, in a gesture, perhaps, to its intermediary or hybrid state as a flying mammal.

The "flower world" references Joy Harjo's "This is My Heart" and "refuse to translate" references Don Mee Choi's anti-imperialist poetics of translation.

"*imagine you're a male garter snake*" is an excerpt of Joan Roughgarden's 'translation' of the common garter snakes' sexual behavior in her book *Evolution's Rainbow: Diversity, Gender, and Sexuality in Nature and People*. The Arabic is my translation of the material into a love poem. Roughgarden's influence appears directly and indirectly across *cue*.

"and my heart has become receptive to every image" is borrowed from Ibn 'Arabi. *cue* was composed as I was reading about Ibn 'Arabi. Especially relevant here are Nuzha Bourada's book *Al-Onutha Fi Fikr Ibn Arabi*, Sadiyya Shaikh's *Sufi Narratives of Intimacy:*

Ibn 'Arabī, Gender, and Sexuality, and Michael Sells's *Mystical Languages of Unsaying*. In a video on the Ibn 'Arabi Society website, scholar Pablo Benito describes the concept of "the journey of the heart," in which he traces Ibn 'Arabi's linguistic derivations and poetic juxtapositions in the line of poetry لقد صار قلبي قابلا كل صورة. If the heart is to mystic transformation a hospitable organ of reception, it does away with the supremacy of orthodox claims to knowledge.

Crow and cockerel's story I translated (with stylistic liberties) from al-Nuwayri's compendium. I came to the text via Elias Muhanna's abridged translation, *The Ultimate Ambition in the Arts of Erudition: A Compendium of Knowledge from the Classical Islamic World*. Further influences and quotes from both the Arabic and the English appear in *cue*.

"you may not know that we're there but we are" blends a line from a testimony in *Bareed Mista3jil* with lines from al-Tifashi's book *Nuzhat al-Albab Fi Ma La Yowjad Fi Kitab* (quoted also by Samar Habib in *Female Homosexuality in the Middle East: Histories and Representations*) and with a line from Roughgarden's *Evolution's Rainbow*.

"plan(e)t—" borrows language from Bernd Rosslenbroich's essay "The Notion of Progress in Evolutionary Biology—The Unresolved Problem and an Empirical Suggestion" published in *Biology and Philosophy*.

cue includes quotes from Tarek El-Ariss' essay "Playing House in the Studio of Hashem El Madani" which appeared in *Camerawork: A Journal of Photographic Arts*, Chad Elias' interview "The Libidinal Archive: A Conversation with Akram Zaatari" in the *Tate Papers*, Gayatri Gopinath's "Queer Visual Excavations: Akram Zaatari, Hashem El Madani, and the Reframing of History in Lebanon" in *Journal of Middle East Women's Studies*, Ashitha's Nagesh's "Reflection in Water: Interview with Akram Zaatari," and *On Photography, People, and Modern Times*, a film by Akram Zaatari.

Erasures are of Michel Foucault's chapter "Classifying" in *The Order of Things*.

ACKNOWLEDGMENTS

Many thanks to Akram Zaatari and the Arab Image Foundation for granting me permission to reprint the photographs from Hashem El Madani's collection.

The images' captions, in the order of their appearance are:

> Najm (left) and Asmar (right). Studio Shehrazade, Saida, Lebanon, 1950s.
>
> Ahmad el Abed, a tailor. Madani's parents' home, the studio, Saida, Lebanon, 1948–1953.
>
> Ahmad el Abed, and his friend Rajab Arna'out. Madani's parents' home, the studio, Saida, Lebanon, 1948–53.
>
> Anonymous. Madani's parents' home, the studio, Saida, Lebanon, 1948–53.
>
> A fisherman with his daughters. Saqqa family house, Saida, Lebanon, 1948–1953.
>
> Anonymous. Studio Shehrazade, Saida, Lebanon, early 1960s.
>
> Reesh. Studio Shehrazade, Saida, Lebanon, late 1960s.
>
> Anonymous. Studio Shehrazade, Saida, Lebanon, early 1970s.
>
> Baqari's wife. Studio Shehrazade, Saida, Lebanon, 1957.

Thanks to the following journals and organizations that have published poems from this manuscript, sometimes in a different iteration or under a different title:

> "it has been said in the thieving," "(t)here from birth," "we," "no layoff from this," "in our language," *Oxeye Reader: Milwaukee, Wisconsin*, edited by Jenny Gropp and Laura Solomon, Oxeye Press, 2024.
>
> "[it has been said in the thieving]" *Bennington Review*, vol. 12, 2023.
>
> "stuck truck black," *We Call to the Eye & the Night: Love Poems by Writers of Arab Descent*, edited and with an introduction by Zeina Hashem Beck and Hala Alyan, Persea Books, 2023.
>
> "a plan(e)t," *Cordite Poetry Review*, May 2023.
>
> "we" and "حارة," *Mītra: Revue d'art et de littérature*, vol. 5, 2021.

"سلوى" and "we," *Fence*, vol. 37, Winter 2021.

"سلوى," Woodland Pattern Book Center's Milwaukee Poem-a-Day, curated by Mauricio Kilwein Guevara, 2021.

"سلوى," Amtrak Poetry in New York City by the Flow Chart Foundation, January 2021.

"[you may not know that we're there but we are you]" *Under a Warm Green Linden*, vol. 9, June 2020.

from "dear a—an essay," *Boyfriend Village / Black Warrior Review*, December 2019.

"mammals—" *Colorado Review*, vol. 45, no. 3, 2018.

"poem," *Oxidant | Engine*, vol.1, 2016.

Gratitude

For mama and baba and Bassel and Muna and the whole familia, and our late nana and tetas and jidotos.

For Hana and Naim, in everything I do, I hope always lives a small gift for you. For Eliana, Haneen, Sari, and Omar. For Shanae, Rania, Peter, Hadeel, Samer, Rand, Natalie, Randa, Sarah, and Nidal.

For Brenda Cárdenas and Kumkum Sangari, without your encouragement and generosity this book would not have been possible. For Kimberly Blaeser, Mauricio Kilwein Guevara, Xin Huang, and Anna McGinty.

For your generous feedback and lovely conversations: Tala Issa, Thoraya El-Rayyes, Marcia Lynx Qualey.

For Milwaukee's friends and writers: Ae Hee Lee, David Kruger, Ghassan Zeineddine, Yasmine Lamloum, Gurkirat Sekhon, Loretta McCormick, and Peter Burzyński.

For Laura Solomon, Jenny Gropp, and Mike Wendt. For Woodland Pattern.

For Alyse Knorr, Kate Partridge, and Daniel D'Angelo.

For Francine Goh, Yan Xin Lee, Mun Yuk Chin, and Lindsey Weber.

For Kwame Dawes and the team at the African Poetry Book Fund and *Prairie Schooner*.

For Soham Patel, for your inimitable, beautiful spirit and your editorial generosity. And for all the wonderful editors and associates at the *Georgia Review* and UGA Press, especially Gerald Maa, my deep appreciation.

Georgia Review Books

What Persists: Selected Essays on Poetry from The Georgia Review, *1988–2014*, by Judith Kitchen

Conscientious Thinking: Making Sense in an Age of Idiot Savants, by David Bosworth

Stargazing in the Atomic Age, by Anne Goldman

Divine Fire, poems by David Woo

Hong Kong without Us: A People's Poetry, edited by the Bauhinia Project

Hysterical Water, poems by Hannah Baker Saltmarsh

This Impermanent Earth: Environmental Writing from The Georgia Review, edited by Douglas Carlson and Soham Patel

GAZE BACK, poems by Marylyn Tan

Natural History, poems by José Watanabe, translated by Michelle Har Kim

The Harm Fields, poems by David Lloyd

Tripas, poems by Brandon Som

Presence: A Novel, by Brenda Iijima

cue: poems, by Siwar Masannat